The Bread Machine Cookbook

All the Best Recipes in One Book
Fresh & Crispy Homemade Bread

Joanna Cooper

TABLE OF CONTENT

INTRODUCTION

Welcome to the world of bread baking made easy! With a dependable bread machine at home, you can skip the rolled-up sleeves, clouds of flour, and sticky countertops and go right to the final product—a beautiful, aromatic, incredible-tasting loaf of home- made bread. You won't even have to do a lot of clean-up afterwards; you will only have to wash a bread pan and a tiny blade.

We have handpicked most popular and at the same time not difficult recipes. Most recipes in this book can be tweaked easily to suit your personal choice. You can substitute or altogether remove any Ingredients (of course except the main ingredient) that you don't have or not liked. Although all recipes as it is are tasted and found to please most people taste bud. What you are waiting for?

Finally, with this cookbook you will find an assortment of recipes to please every palate. From the very simple white and wheat breads, to sweet flavors and interesting combinations, bread-making has never been so easy or mouthwatering!

If you haven't made use of all the advantages your bread machine has to offer you, then now is your chance to start your own bread journey with these recipes that are tried, tasted and tested.

Happy baking!

CHAPTER 1: WHAT IS A BREAD MACHINE?

A bread machine is a kitchen appliance used to bake bread at home. A small oven encompasses a bread pan and paddle and is typically controlled with settings to customize cooking times and types of bread.

Advantages of Using A Bread Machine

- **Freshly baked homemade bread**-The list of benefits is seemingly endless; the taste of something homemade is typically superior to anything store bought and there's the added advantage of knowing the ingredients used – nothing artificial in here. This is especially important for those with allergies.

- **Less mess to clean up** as all the ingredients are mixed together in one pan, and with the ease of using the controlled settings, there's no kneading or prolonged wait times.

- A bread machine will knead bread better than you can.

- **Ease of use** - a bread machine is an awesome way to get someone into bread making, it is so easy.

Disadvantages of Using A Bread Machine

- ❖ **Convenience**-Only one loaf of bread can be made at a time, and it may take a few tries to get that "perfect" looking loaf.

- ❖ **Labor**- And while there is less mess to clean up after the machine cannot be put in the dishwasher, it must be cleaned carefully by hand otherwise it may not function correctly afterward.

- ❖ **Kitchen Space** -You will have to consider where the machine can be stored when not in use. In deciding whether a bread machine is for you though.

Basic ingredients used in a bread machine

Flours: bread, all-purpose (unbleached or regular), whole wheat, rye, barley, buckwheat, millet

- ❖ Wholewheat flour, unlike white flour, is ground from the complete wheat berry and thus contains the wheat germ as well as the wheat bran. Avoid using stoneground whole wheat in the bread machine. It is coarser in texture and does not rise as well as regular whole wheat flour in the machine.
- ❖ Rye flour is heavy flour milled from the rye grain. It is low in gluten. You will need to combine it with white or whole wheat flour to produce an acceptable-size loaf. Rye dough is also stickier than other dough.
- ❖ Barley flour is very high in minerals. It contributes a slightly sweet taste and a cake like texture to the dough.
- ❖ Buckwheat flour has a strong, tart, and earthy flavor and lends a grayish color to the finished product. We use it in small quantities because a little goes a long way.
- ❖ Millet flour is ground from whole millet, and when added to bread, gives it a dry taste and texture.
- ❖ Oats have the highest protein and mineral content of all grains. They add that sweet and nutty "country" richness to bread.
- ❖ Bulgur is cracked wheat that has been parboiled and dried for faster cooking. It will absorb liquids more readily than cracked wheat.
- ❖ Bran is the outer covering of the wheat kernel. It is added to bread recipes for texture, flavor, and fiber. Use it sparingly since too much bran doesn't give a pleasant taste.

Liquids: milk or nonfat dry milk powder, buttermilk or dry buttermilk powder
Whole grains: oats, wheat bran, wheat germ, cracked wheat or bulgur, millet
Sweeteners: granulated sugar, dark and light brown sugar, confectioners' sugar, honey, molasses

Fats: margarine or unsalted butter, vegetable and olive oil, shortening

Miscellaneous: yeast, salt, eggs, sour cream, sunflower seeds, oranges, raisins, Parmesan cheese, herbs and spices

Common Abbreviations

cup(s)	C.
tablespoon	tbsp
teaspoon	tsp
ounce	oz.
pound	lb

All units used are standard American measurements

US Cups Measurement

US cups	Amount in Grams	Amount in Ounces
1/2 cup	75g	3 oz
2/3 cup	100g	4 oz
3/4 cup	113g	4 1/2 oz
1 cup	150g	6 oz

CHAPTER 2: BREAD MACHINE RECIPES

1. Basic white bread

Makes: 1 loaf
Total prep time: 1 hour 15 minutes

Ingredients:
- Water ½ to ⅝ cup
- Milk ⅝ cup
- Butter or margarine 1½ tablespoons
- Sugar 3 tablespoons
- Salt 1½ teaspoons
- Bread flour 3 cups
- Active dry yeast 1½ teaspoons

Directions:
- Put all ingredients in the bread pan, using minimal measure of liquid listed in the recipe.
- Select medium Crust setting and press Start.
- Observe the dough as it kneads. Following 5 to 10 minutes, in the event that it seems dry and firm, or if your machine seems as though it's straining to knead, add more liquid 1 tablespoon at a time until dough forms well.
- Once the baking cycle ends, remove bread from pan, and allow to cool before slicing.

2. Gluten Free Bread

Makes: 1 loaf (12 slices)
Total prep time: 4 hours, 50 minutes

Ingredients:

- 2 cups rice flour Potato starch
- ½ cup Tapioca flour
- ½ cup Xanthan gum
- 2 ½ teaspoons ⅔ cup powdered milk or 1/2 non diary substitute
- Salt - 1 ½ teaspoons 1 ½ teaspoons egg substitute (optional)
- Sugar - 3 tablespoons
- Lukewarm water - 1 ⅔ cups
- Dry yeast, granules - 1 ½ tablespoons
- Butter, melted or margarine - 4 tablespoons
- Vinegar - 1 teaspoon
- 3 eggs, room temperature

Directions:

- Add yeast to the bread pan.
- Add all the flours, xanthan/ gum, milk powder, salt, and sugar.
- Beat the eggs, and mix with water, butter, and vinegar.
- Choose white bread setting at medium or use 3-4 hour setting.

3. Potato bread

Makes: 1 loaf (12 slices)
Total prep time: 1 hour, 15 minutes

Ingredients:
- 3/8 cup milk
- 1/4 to 3/8 cup potato water*
- 1 tbsp. Butter or margarine
- 1 tbsp. Sugar
- 1 tsp. Salt
- 2 cups all-purpose flour
- 1/4 cup plain mashed potato, room temperature
- 1 1/2 tsp. Active dry yeast

Directions:
- Using the least amount of the liquid indicated in the recipe, place all the Ingredients in the bread pan. Select medium crust. Press start.
- After 5-10 minutes, observe the dough as it kneads, if you hear straining sounds in your machine or if the dough appears stiff and dry, add 1 tbsp. Liquid at a time until the dough becomes smooth, pliable, soft, and slightly tacky to the touch.
- Remove the bread from the pan after baking. Place on rack and allow to cool for 1 hour before slicing.

note: the amount of liquid you will need to use will depend on the moisture content of your potato.

4. Herb bread

Makes: 1 loaf (12 slices)
Total prep time: 1 hour, 20 minutes

Ingredients:

- 3/4 to 7/8 cup milk
- 1 tbsp. Sugar
- 1 tsp. Salt
- 2 tbsp. Butter or margarine
- 1/3 cup chopped onion
- 2 cups bread flour
- 1/2 tsp. Dried dill
- 1/2 tsp. Dried basil
- 1/2 tsp. Dried rosemary
- 11/2 tsp. Active dry yeast

Directions:

- Using the least amount of the liquid indicated in the recipe, place all the Ingredients in the bread pan. Select medium crus then the rapid bake cycle. Press start.
- After 5-10 minutes, observe the dough as it kneads, if you hear straining sounds in your machine or if the dough appears stiff and dry, add 1 tbsp. Liquid at a time until the dough becomes smooth, pliable, soft, and slightly tacky to the touch.
- Remove the bread from the pan after baking. Place on rack and allow to cool for 1 hour before slicing.

5. Whole-wheat bread

Makes: 1 loaf (12 slices)
Total prep time: 1 hour, 10 minutes

Ingredients:

- 3/4 to 7/8 cup water
- 1 tsp. Salt
- 3 tbsp. Butter or margarine
- 1 tbsp. Sugar
- 11/3 cups whole wheat flour
- 2/3 cups bread flour
- 3 tbsp. Instant potato flakes
- 11/2 tsp. Active dry
  yeast optional:
- 2 tbsp. Vital wheat gluten

Directions:

- Using the least amount of the liquid indicated in the recipe, place all the Ingredients in the bread pan. Select medium crust then the whole wheat cycle. Press start.
- After 5-10 minutes, observe the dough as it kneads, if you hear straining sounds in your machine or if the dough appears stiff and dry, add 1 tbsp. Liquid at a time until the dough becomes smooth, pliable, soft, and slightly tacky to the touch.
- Remove the bread from the pan after baking. Place on rack and allow to cool for 1 hour before slicing.

6. Apple butter wheat bread

Makes: 1 loaf (12 slices)
Total prep time: 1 hour, 15 minutes

Ingredients:

- 5/8 to 3/4 cup water
- 1 tbsp. Butter or margarine
- 3 tbsp. Apple butter
- 1 tsp. Salt
- 1 cup whole wheat flour
- 1 cup all-purpose flour
- 11/2 tsp. Active dry yeast

Directions:

- Using the least amount of the liquid indicated in the recipe, place all the Ingredients in the bread pan. Select medium crust. Press start.
- After 5-10 minutes, observe the dough as it kneads, if you hear straining sounds in your machine or if the dough appears stiff and dry, add 1 tbsp. Liquid at a time until the dough becomes smooth, pliable, soft, and slightly tacky to the touch.
- Remove the bread from the pan after baking. Place on rack and allow to cool for 1 hour before slicing.

7. Sauerkraut rye bread

Makes: 1 loaf (12 slices)
Total prep time: 1 hour, 15 minutes

Ingredients:

- 1/2 to 5/8 cup water
- 1/2 cup sauerkraut, well-drained, squeezed, and chopped
- 1 tbsp. Butter or margarine
- 1 tbsp. Molasses
- 1 tbsp. Dark brown sugar
- 1 tsp. Salt
- 11/3cups bread flour
- 2/3 cups rye flour
- 2 tsp. Caraway seeds
- 2 tsp. Active dry yeast optional:
- 11/2 tbsp. Vital wheat gluten

Directions:

- Using the least amount of the liquid indicated in the recipe, place all the Ingredients in the bread pan. Select medium crust. Press start.
- After 5-10 minutes, observe the dough as it kneads, if you hear straining sounds in your machine or if the dough appears stiff and dry, add 1 tbsp. Liquid at a time until the dough becomes smooth, pliable, soft, and slightly tacky to the touch.
- Remove the bread from the pan after baking. Place on rack and allow to cool for 1hour before slicing.

8. Banana bread

Makes: 1 loaf (12 slices)
Total prep time: 1 hour, 40 minutes

Ingredients:

- 1 tsp. Baking powder
- 1/2 tsp. Baking soda
- 2 bananas, peeled and halved lengthwise
- 2 cups all-purpose flour
- 2 eggs
- 3 tbsp. Vegetable oil
- 3/4 cup white sugar

Directions:

- Put all the Ingredients in the bread pan. Select dough setting. Start and mix for about 3-5 minutes, or until the Ingredients are combined thoroughly and the bananas are mashed. When needed, use a rubber spatula to push the dough from sides of the bread pan.
- After 3-5 minutes, press stop. Do not continue to mix. Smooth out the top of the dough
- Using the spatula and then select bake. Start and bake for about 50 minutes. After 50 minutes, insert a toothpick into the top center to test doneness. If the toothpick comes out clean when you remove it, it is done. If you see batter, continue to bake for 10-15 minutes more.
- Test the loaf again. When the bread is completely baked, remove the pan from the machine and let the bread remain in the pan for10 minutes. Remove bread and cool in wire rack.

9. Onion, garlic, cheese bread

Makes: 1 loaf
Total prep time: 50 minutes

Ingredients:

- 3 tbsp. Dried minced onion
- 3 cups bread flour
- 2 tsp. Garlic powder
- 2 tsp. Active dry yeast
- 2 tbsp. White sugar
- 2 tbsp. Margarine
- 2 tbsp. Dry milk powder
- 1 cup shredded sharp cheddar cheese
- 1 1/8 cups warm water
- 1 1/2 tsp. Salt

Directions:

- In the order suggested by the manufacturer, put the flour, water, powdered milk, margarine or butter, salt, and yeast in the bread pan.
- Press the basic cycle with light crust. When the sound alerts or as directed by the manufacturer, add 2 tsp. Of the onion flakes, the garlic powder, and all of the shredded cheese.
- After the last kneed, sprinkle the remaining onion flakes over the dough.
- Enjoy fresh and hot.

10.Brownie bread

Makes: 1 loaf
Total prep time: 1 hour, 15 minutes

Ingredients:

- 1 egg
- 1 egg yolk
- 1 tsp. Salt
- 1/2 cup boiling water
- 1/2 cup cocoa powder, unsweetened
- 1/2 cup warm water
- 2 1/2 tsp. Active dry yeast
- 2 tbsp. Vegetable oil
- 2 tsp. White sugar
- 2/3 cup white sugar
- 3 cups bread flour

Directions:

- Put the cocoa powder in a small bow. Pour boiling water and dissolve the cocoa powder.
- Put the warm water, yeast and the 2 tsp. White sugar in another bowl. Dissolve yeast and sugar. Let stand for about 10 minutes, or until the mix is creamy.
- Place the cocoa mix, the yeast mix, the flour, the 2/3 cup white sugar, the salt, the vegetable, and the egg in the bread pan. Select basic bread cycle. Press start.

11. Pumpernickel Bread

Makes: 1 loaf
Total prep time: 2 Hours 10 Minutes

Ingredients:

- 1 1/8 cups warm water
- 1 ½ tablespoons vegetable oil
- 1/3 cup molasses
- 3 tablespoons cocoa
- 1 tablespoon caraway seed (optional)
- 1 ½ tsp salt
- 1 ½ cups of bread flour
- 1 cup of rye flour
- 1 cup whole wheat flour
- 1 ½ tablespoons of vital wheat gluten (optional)
- 2 ½ tsp of bread machine yeast

Directions:

- Add all ingredients to bread machine pan.
- Choose basic bread cycle.
- Take bread out to cool and enjoy!

guettes

Servings: 12
Total prep time: 2 hours, 5 minutes

Ingredients:

- 1 cup water
- 2 cups bread flour
- 1 tablespoon white sugar
- 1 tsp salt
- 1 ½ tsp bread machine yeast
- 1 egg yolk
- 1 tablespoon water

Directions:

- Bread Machine: Add 1 cup water, bread flour, sugar, salt and yeast to the bread pan. Choose the dough cycle.
- Grease a bowl and when finished put dough inside, then cover.
- Let sit and rise for about 30 minutes in a warm place.
- Bread should be doubled in size.

13. Egg Bread

Makes: 1 loaf
Total prep time: 3 hours, 5 minutes

Ingredients:

- 1/2 cup milk
- 1 large egg
- 1 tablespoon butter OR margarine, cut up
- 3/4 teaspoon salt
- 2 cups bread flour
- 1 tablespoon sugar
- 1 ½ tsp bread machine yeast
- 1 tsp finely shredded lemon or orange peel

Directions:

- Add all ingredients to bread machine pan.
- Choose basic bread cycle with medium crust setting.

14. English muffin Bread

Makes: 1 loaf
Total prep time: 5 hrs, 55 min

Ingredients:

- 1 teaspoon vinegar
- 1/4 cup (in summer) OR 1/3 cup (in winter) water
- 1 cup lukewarm milk
- 2 tablespoons butter or vegetable oil
- 1 ½ tsp salt
- 1 ½ tsp sugar
- ½ tsp baking powder
- 3 ½ cups unbleached all - purpose flour
- 2 ¼ tsp instant yeast

Directions:

- Add all of the ingredients into pan.
- Add water depending on season
- Choose basic white bread setting, light crust.
- Check on the dough in the second kneading cycle. It should be soft and smooth, and a little bit sticky.
- Add additional flour or water as needed to get this consistency. In order to obtain the texture of an English muffin, take out the dough during final kneading or before the final rise
- Roll the dough in cornmeal, and then put back into machine. After the final rise and baking, remove finished bread and cool.

15. Scandinavian rye bread

Makes: 1 loaf
Total prep time: 3 hours, 15 minutes

Ingredients:

- Water 1⅛ cups
- Oil 2 tablespoons
- Dark karo syrup
- ½ cup salt
- ½ teaspoon all-purpose flour
- 3 cups rye flour
- 1 cup grated orange rind
- 2 teaspoons anise seed
- 1 teaspoon cardamom
- 1 teaspoon
- Active dry yeast

Directions:

- Place dough Ingredients in bread pan and select dough setting. Press start.
- When the dough has risen long enough, the machine will beep. Turn off bread machine, remove bread pan, and turn out dough onto a lightly floured countertop or cutting board.
- Grease a large baking sheet. Gently shape dough into a smooth ball. Flatten slightly and place on prepared baking sheet. With a sharp knife, slash the loaf with an x or # on the top.
- Cover and let rise in a warm oven 45 to 60 minutes until doubled in size. (hint: to warm oven slightly, turn oven on warm setting for 1 minute, then turn it off, and place covered dough in oven to rise. Remove pan from oven before preheating.)
- Preheat oven to 350° f. Bake for 40 to 45 minutes.
- Remove from oven, place on cake rack, and allow to cool 1 hour before slicing.

16. Italian Panettone in Bread Machine

Makes: 1 loaf
Total prep time: 3 hours, 15 minutes

Ingredients:

- Buttermilk 2 cups
- Molasses 1 cup
- Whole wheat flour 1 cup
- Rye flour 1 cup
- Cornmeal 1 cup
- Salt 1 teaspoon b
- Baking soda 2 teaspoons
- Raisins (optional) 1 cup

Directions:

- Place all Ingredients in bread pan, select cake/quick bread setting, and press start.
- Make sure the batter is well mixed before baking begins. It's so thick, you may need to give it a stir or two with a spatula.
- When the bread starts baking, set a timer for 60 minutes. After 60 minutes of baking, test the bread for doneness with a long wooden or bamboo skewer. If the skewer comes out clean and the bread is firm, shut off the machine and remove the bread. (we've learned the hard way that some machines have an overly long baking cycle for cakes and quick breads, so it's best to check them early.)
- Place the bread on a cake rack and allow it to cool before slicing.

17. Irish bread

Makes: 1 loaf
Total prep time: 2 hour

Ingredients:

- Egg 2
- Vanilla 1 teaspoon
- Sour cream 2 cups
- Sugar 1 cup
- Bread flour 5 cups
- Baking soda 1½ teaspoons
- Active dry yeast 2½ teaspoons
- Raisins 1 cup

Directions:

- Place all Ingredients except raisins in bread pan, select light crust setting and raisin/nut cycle. Press start.
- At the beep, add raisins.
- After the baking cycle ends, remove bread from pan, place on cake rack, and allow to cool 1 hour before slicing.

18.Blueberry bread

Makes: 1 loaf
Total prep time: 3 hours, 15 minutes

Ingredients:

- Water 1⅛ to 1¼ cups
- Cream cheese, softened 6 ounces
- Butter or margarine 2 tablespoons
- Sugar ¼ cup
- Salt 2 teaspoons
- Bread flour 4½ cups
- Grated lemon peel 1½ teaspoons
- Cardamom 2 teaspoons
- Nonfat dry milk 2 tablespoons
- Red star brand active dry yeast 2½ teaspoons
- Dried blueberries ⅔ cup

Directions:

- Place all Ingredients except dried blueberries in bread pan, using the least amount of liquid listed in the recipe. Select light crust setting and raisin/nut cycle. Press start.
- Observe the dough as it kneads. After 5 to 10 minutes, if it appears dry and stiff or if your ma- chine sounds as if it's straining to knead it, add more liquid 1 tablespoon at a time until dough forms a smooth, soft, pliable ball that is slightly tacky to the touch.
- At the beep, add the dried blueberries.
- After the baking cycle ends, remove bread from pan, place on cake rack, and allow to cool 1 hour before slicing. Creative suggestion: substitute any dried fruit for the blueberries. Use grated orange peel instead of grated lemon peel.

19. Portuguese sweet bread

Makes: 1 loaf
Total prep time: 1 hours, 10 minutes

Ingredients:

- Water ¾ to ⅞ cup
- Egg 3
- Butter or margarine 6 tablespoons
- Sugar ½ cup
- Salt 1½ teaspoons
- Bread flour 4¼ cups
- Nonfat dry milk powder 3 tablespoons
- Active dry yeast 2½ teaspoons

Directions:

- Place all Ingredients in bread pan, using the least amount of liquid listed in the recipe. Select
- Light crust setting and sweet bread cycle. Press start.
- Observe the dough as it kneads. After 5 to 10 minutes, if it appears dry and stiff or if your ma- chine sounds as if it's straining to knead it, add more liquid 1 tablespoon at a time until dough forms a smooth, soft, pliable ball that is slightly tacky to the touch.
- After the baking cycle ends, remove bread from pan, place on cake rack, and allow to cool 1 hour before slicing.

20.Savory olive bread

Makes: 1 loaf
Total prep time: 2 hours, 15 minutes

Ingredients:
- Water ¾ to ⅞ cup
- Egg 2
- Olive oil ¼ cup
- Sugar 2 teaspoons
- Salt 1 teaspoon
- Bread flour 2⅔ cups
- Semolina flour 1⅓ cups
- Red star brand active dry yeast 2½ teaspoons
- Chopped and pitted green olives, drained 1 cup
- Finely diced cooked ham ½ cup
- Chopped onion ½ cup

Directions:
- Place all Ingredients except olives, ham, and onion in bread pan, using the least amount of liquid listed in the recipe. Select medium crust setting and raisin/nut cycle. Press start.
- Observe the dough as it kneads. After 5 to 10 minutes, if it appears dry and stiff or if your ma- chine sounds as if it's straining to knead it, add more liquid 1 tablespoon at a time until dough forms a smooth, soft, pliable ball that is slightly tacky to the touch.
- At the beep, add the olives, ham, and onion.
- After the baking cycle ends, remove bread from pan, place on cake rack, and allow to cool 1 hour before slicing. Crust: medium bake cycle: raisin/nut optional bake cycles: standard/ whole wheat

21. Irish bread

Makes: 4-6
Total prep time: 2 hours, 15 minutes

Ingredients:
- 3 cups cake flour, sifted
- 1 cup all-purpose flour, sifted
- ½ tablespoon baking soda
- 1 teaspoon salt
- 1 ½ cup buttermilk

Directions:
- In a mixing bowl, mix all dry Ingredients well and add the buttermilk. Stir well using a wooden spoon to form dough that is a little rough in texture.
- Preheat oven to 450°f and transfer the dough to a lightly floured table and lightly knead dough. Add more flour if dough is still sticky and remember not to over knead.
- Lightly flour a baking sheet and transfer dough on it, form dough into a loaf. Make a shallow slice with an x form and bake it in the oven. Bake for 10 minutes and reduce the heat to 400°f. Bake for another 30 minutes and it is done when the loaf starts to brown, or produce a shallow sound when knocked gently.
- Transfer to a rack and let it rest for a while before slicing.

22.Buttermilk Bread

Makes: 1 Loaf
Total prep time: 1 hour

Ingredients:
- 1 ¼ cups warm buttermilk
- 2 tablespoons butter, softened
- 3 cups all-purpose flour
- 3 tablespoons sugar
- 1 tsp salt
- 2 tsp yeast

Directions:
- Add all ingredients in bread machine.
- Choose basic bread setting cycle.
- Take bread out to cool and enjoy!

23.Italian Breadsticks

Makes: 24 breadsticks
Total prep time: 1 hour

Ingredients:

- 1 cup room temperature water
- 3 tablespoons butter- softened
- 1 ½ teaspoons salt
- 3 cups bread flour
- 2 tablespoons sugar
- 1 tsp Italian seasoning
- 1 tsp garlic powder
- 2 ¼ tsp active dry yeast

Topping:

- 1 tablespoon butter
- 1 tablespoon fresh grated Parmesan

Directions: Bread Machine

- In machine pan, all ingredients.
- Choose dough setting.
- Check on dough every 5 minutes and add flour or water if necessary.
- Dough cycle completes after an estimated hour and a half .

24.Italian bread

Makes: 2-3
Total prep time: 1 hour 30 minutes

Ingredients:

- Water
- 1⅜ to 1½ cups olive oil
- 2 tablespoons salt
- 1½ teaspoons bread flour
- 4 cups vital wheat gluten (opti onal)
- 4 tablespoons red star brand
- Active dry yeast 2 teaspoons

Directions:

- Place all Ingredients in bread pan, using the least amount of liquid listed in the recipe. Select medium crust setting, the french bread cycle, and press start.
- Observe the dough as it kneads. After 5 to 10 minutes, if it appears dry and stiff or if your ma- chine sounds as if it's straining to knead it, add more liquid 1 tablespoon at a time until dough forms a smooth, soft, pliable ball that is slightly tacky to the touch.
- After the baking cycle ends, remove bread from pan, place on cake rack, and allow to cool 1 hour before slicing.

25. Tuscan bread

Makes: 2-3
Total prep time: 1 hour 30 minutes

Ingredients:

- Water 1½ to 1⅝ cups
- Olive oil 3 tablespoons
- Sugar 4 teaspoons
- Bread flour 4 cups
- Red star brand active dry yeast 2 teaspoons

Directions:

- Place all Ingredients in bread pan, using the least amount of liquid listed in the recipe. Select dark crust setting and french bread cycle. Press start.
- Observe the dough as it kneads. After 5 to 10 minutes, if it appears dry and stiff or if your ma- chine sounds as if it's straining to knead it, add more liquid 1 tablespoon at a time until dough forms a smooth, soft, pliable ball that is slightly tacky to the touch.
- After the baking cycle ends, remove bread from pan, place on cake rack, and allow to cool 1 hour before slicing.

26. Oat Bread

Makes: 2-3
Total prep time: 1 hour 30 minutes

Ingredients:

- Oats 1 cup
- Water 1⅜ to 1½ cups
- Butter or margarine 2 tablespoons
- Honey ¼ cup
- Salt 2 teaspoons
- Bread flour 3 cups red star brand
- Active dry yeast 2½ teaspoons

Directions:

- Place all Ingredients in bread pan, using the least amount of liquid listed in the recipe. Select medium crust setting and press start.
- Observe the dough as it kneads. After 5 to 10 minutes, if it appears dry and stiff or if your machine sounds as if it's straining to knead it, add more liquid 1 tablespoon at a time until dough forms a smooth, soft, pliable ball that is slightly tacky to the touch.
- After the baking cycle ends, remove bread from pan, place on cake rack, and allow to cool 1 hour before slicing.

27.Cinnamon buns

Makes: 2-3
Total prep time: 1 hour 30 minutes

Ingredients:

- 4 tbsp. Water
- 4 tbsp. Melted butter
- 4 cups bread flour
- 2 1/4 tsp. Bread machine yeast
- 1/2 tsp. Salt
- 1/2 (3.5 oz.) Package instant vanilla pudding mix
- 1 tbsp. White sugar
- 1 egg, beaten
- 1 cup milk topping:
- 2 tsp. Ground cinnamon
- 1/2 cup butter, softened
- 1 cup packed brown sugar
- 1/4 cup raisins
- 1/4 cup chopped walnuts

Frosting:

- 4 tbsp. Butter, softened
- 1 tsp. Vanilla extract
- 1 tsp. Milk
- 1 1/2 cups confectioners' sugar

Directions:

- In the order suggested by the manufacturer, put the dough Ingredients in the bread pan. Select dough cycle. Press start. Remove dough when the cycle is complete. Knead for about 3-5 minutes, and then roll out into a large rectangle.
- Mix the topping Ingredients. Spread it over the flattened dough, and then sprinkle with the raisins and walnuts, if desired. Starting at the widest end, roll the dough into a log. Pinch the seams to seal.
- Grease a 9x13-inch pan. Cut the log into 1/2 to 1-inch slices. Place the cut logs in the prepared pan. Place the pan in a draft-free space and let rise until doubled.
- Preheat oven to 350f or 175c.
- Transfer the pan to the preheated oven and bake for about 15-20 minutes.
- Mix the frosting Ingredients. Spread over baked warm cinnamon rolls.

28.Bread machine pizza dough

Makes: 2-3
Total prep time: 45 minutes

Ingredients:

- 2 tbsp. Sugar
- 2 tbsp. Butter
- 2 1/4 tsp. Yeast
- 2 1/2 cups all-purpose flour
- 1 tsp. Salt
- 1 cup flat beer
- Olive oil

Directions:

- In the order suggested by the manufacturer, put all the Ingredients in the bread machine, select dough setting. Press start.
- Prepare your pizza pan.
- Remove dough when the cycle is complete and press or roll to cover the prepared pizza pan. Lightly brush with olive oil. Cover. Let stand for 15 minutes.
- Preheat oven to 400f or 200c.
- Spread your favorite pizza sauce over the dough and top with your favorite toppings.
- Bake for about 24 minutes or until the crust is lightly brown.

29. Sweet dinner rolls

Makes: 2-3
Total prep time: 1 hour 30 minutes

Ingredients:

- 3 3/4 cups all-purpose flour
- 1/4 cup butter, softened
- 1/3 cup white sugar
- 1/3 cup butter, softened
- 1/2 cup warm water
- 1/2 cup warm milk
- 1 tsp. Salt
- 1 pack (1/4 oz.) Active dry yeast
- 1 egg

Directions:

- In the order suggested by the manufacturer, place flour, milk, water, 1/3 cup butter, egg, salt, sugar, and yeast in the bread pan. Select dough/knead and then first rise cycle. Press start.
- Remove dough when the cycle is complete and rest on a lightly floured surface. Divide the dough into half. Roll each half into a 12-inch circle. Spread the entire 1/4 cup butter over the dough circles.
- Cut each circle into 8 wedges. Starting at the wide end, roll the wedges gently but tightly.
- Point-side down, place the rolled wedges in an uncreased cookie sheet. Cover it with clean towel and put in a warm place. Let rise for 1 hour.
- Preheat oven to 400 f or 200 degrees c.
- Bake for about 10-15 minutes, or until golden brown.

30. Honey wheat rolls

Makes: 12-13
Total prep time: 1 hour 30 minutes

Dough Ingredients:
- 1 1/4 cups warm milk
- 1 1/4 tsp. Bread machine yeast
- 1 cup whole wheat flour
- 1 egg, beaten
- 1/4 cup honey
- 2 3/4 cups bread flour
- 2 tbsp. Butter, melted
- 2 tbsp. Butter, softened
- 3/4 tsp. Salt

Directions:
- In the order suggested by the manufacturer, put all the Ingredients in the bread machine, select dough setting. Press start.
- Remove dough when the cycle is complete and rest on a lightly floured surface.
- Lightly grease two cookie sheets. Roll the dough into 3/4-inch thickness. Using a 3 to 4-inch biscuit cutter, cut out the rolls. Place the cut rolls in prepared cookie sheets, cover, and let rise for about 1 hour, or until doubled.
- Preheat oven to 350f or 175c.
- Bake for about 10-15 minutes. When done, brush with melted butter.

31. French Braided brioche

Makes: 2-3
Total prep time: 1 hour

Ingredients:

- 1/2 tsp. Active dry yeast
- 1/3 cup warm water
- 1/4 cup white sugar
- 2 egg yolks
- 3 1/3 cups all-purpose flour
- 3 eggs
- 3/4 cup butter, softened for brushing:
- 2 tbsp. Water
- 1 egg white

Directions:

- In the order listed, measure the dough Ingredients into the bread pan. Select the dough cycle. Press start. Remove dough when the cycle is complete and rest on a lightly floured surface. Knead 5-10 times.
- Line a baking sheet with parchment paper.
- Separate the dough into 2-3 pieces. Using your hands, roll the dough into strips. Twist or braid the strips together. Transfer into prepared baking sheet and place in a warm place to double.
- Preheat oven to 350f or 175c.
- Whisk the water and the egg white together and brush on the top of the dough.
- Bake for 20 minutes until golden brown.

32.Ciabatta means "slipper" in Italian.

Makes: 3 loaves
Total prep time: 50 minutes

Ingredients:
- 1⅝ cups Water
- Sourdough starter ⅔ cup
- Salt 1½ teaspoons
- Bread flour 4 to 4¼ cups
- Nonfat dry milk powder 2 teaspoons
- Active dry yeast 2½ teaspoons

Directions:
- Place dough Ingredients in bread pan, select dough setting, and press start.
- When the dough has risen long enough, the machine will beep. Turn off bread machine, remove bread pan, and turn out dough onto a heavily floured countertop or cutting board. This is a very wet, sticky dough. Sprinkle some flour on top of dough as well.
- Grease a large baking sheet. For the small recipe with a sharp knife, divide dough into 2 pieces. Handling the dough as little as possible, use a spatula or dough scraper to shape the 2 loaves into rough 4×8-inch ovals. For the medium recipe with a sharp knife, divide dough into 2 pieces. Handling the dough as little as possible, use a spatula or dough scraper to shape the 2 loaves into rough 4×10-inch ovals.For the large recipe with a sharp knife, divide dough into 3 pieces.

Directions:

Handling the dough as little as possible, use a spatula or dough scraper to shape the 3 loaves into rough 4×10-inch ovals.

- Transfer loaves with spatula to prepared baking sheet. Cover and let rise in a warm oven 30 to 45 minutes until almost doubled in size. (hint: to warm oven slightly, turn oven on warm setting for 1 minute, then turn it off, and place covered dough in oven to rise. Remove pan from oven before preheating.)
- Preheat oven to 425°f. Bake for 25 to 30 minutes until dark brown.
- Remove from oven and cool on a rack 1 hour before slicing.

33.Brown Bread

Makes: 1 loaf
Total prep time: 4 hour 20 minutes

Ingredients:

- 1 ½ cups water
- 3/4 cup rolled oats
- 1/3 cup molasses
- 2 tablespoons shortening
- 1 ½ teaspoon salt
- 3 cups flour
- 2 tsp yeast

Directions:

- Add all ingredients to bread machine.
- Choose the whole wheat setting.
- Take bread out to cool and enjoy!

34.Sour Cream Bread

Makes: 1 loaf
Total prep time: 2 hour 35 minutes

Ingredients:
- 2 tablespoons water
- 1 ½ cups sour cream, softened to room temperature
- 3 ¾ cups flour
- 1 ½ tablespoons packed brown sugar
- 1 tsp salt
- 2 ¼ tsp yeast

Directions:
- Add all ingredients to bread pan.
- Select rapid cook setting on medium crust

35. Whole Wheat Bread

Makes: 1 loaf
Total prep time: 10 minutes
Bake: 3 hours

Ingredients:

- 1 ½ cups water
- 3 tablespoons honey
- 2 tablespoons butter or margarine
- 1 ½ teaspoons salt
- 4 cups whole wheat flour
- 3 tablespoons nonfat dry milk powder
- 1 tablespoon wheat gluten
- 2 teaspoons Bread Machine Yeast

Directions:

- Add all ingredients to bread machine pan
- Select basic/white bread or whole wheat bread Select medium-normal color.
- Select 2 -lb. setting.
- Bake according to manufacturer directions.

36. Butter bread rolls

Makes: 24 rolls
Total prep time: 50 minutes

Ingredients:
- 1 cup warm milk
- ½ cup butter or ½ cup margarine, softened
- ¼ cup sugar
- 2 eggs
- 1 ½ teaspoons salt
- 4 cups bread flour
- 2 ¼ teaspoons active dry yeast

Directions:
- In bread machine pan, put all ingredients in order suggested by manufacturer.
- Select dough setting.
- When cycle is completed, turn dough onto a lightly floured surface.
- Divide dough into 24 portions.
- Shape dough into balls.
- Place in a greased 13 inch by 9 inch baking pan.
- Cover and let rise in a warm place for 30-45 minutes.
- Bake at 350 degrees for 13-16 minutes or until golden brown.

37.Sourdough bread

Makes: 1 ½ loaves
Total prep time: 50 minutes

Ingredients:	Directions:
• ¾ cup water	• Add ingredients in the order given above.
• 1 cup sourdough starter	• Bake on "basic" bread setting.
• 1 ½ teaspoons salt	
• 2 ⅔ cups bread flour	
• 1 ½ teaspoons yeast.	

38.Parsley bread

Makes: 1 loaf
Total prep time: 50 minutes

Ingredients:

- 1 ¼ cups water
- 1 ½ tablespoons olive oil
- 1 teaspoon salt
- 3 ½ cups bread flour
- 2 teaspoons sugar
- 1 tablespoon dried parsley flakes
- ¼ cup grated parmesan cheese
- 2 teaspoons dried onion flakes
- ½ teaspoon dried basil
- ½ teaspoon garlic powder or 1 teaspoon dried garlic flakes
- 2 teaspoons active dry yeast

Directions:

- All ingredients should be at room temperature.
- Add ingredients as your bread machine directs or add all liquid ingredients to bread pan.
- Add all dry ingredients except yeast to bread pan.
- Make a well in dry ingredients and carefully add yeast.
- Choose the "French" bread setting.
- Choose your crust color, if applicable.
- Press start!

39. Honey spelt bread

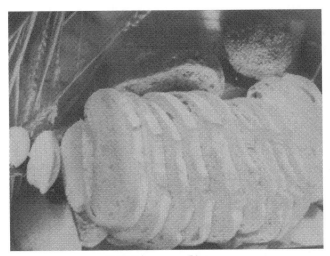

Makes: 1 slices
Total prep time: 50 minutes

Ingredients:

- 1 1/4 cups warm water
- 1 1/2 teaspoons salt
- 2 tablespoons canola oil
- 3 tablespoons honey
- 3 1/2 cups whole grain spelt flour
- 1 3/4 teaspoons bread machine yeast

Directions:

- Put the ingredients into your machine in the listed order.
- Choose setting on bread machine: light crust, 1.5 pound loaf, either the rapid wheat or Whole wheat settings work just fine, depending on how much time you have.
- After the flour has been added, make a depression in the flour to hold the yeast until mixing begins.

40.Fail proof bread

Makes: 2 loaves
Total prep time: 50 minutes

Ingredients:

- 3 ½ cups Bread flour
- 1 teaspoon Salt
- 1 (1/4 ounce) package of active dry yeast
- 1 ¼ cups Warm water

Directions:

- Place ingredients in bread machine according to manufacturer's directions.
- Start machine on dough setting.
- When dough cycle is complete, remove dough with floured hands and cut in half on Floured surface.
- Take each half of dough and roll to make a loaf about 12 inches long in the shape of French bread.
- Place on greased baking sheet and cover with a towel.
- Let rise until doubled, about 1 hour.
- Preheat oven to 450°.
- Bake for 15 to 20 minutes or until golden brown, turning pan around once halfway during baking.
- Remove baked loaves to wire racks to cool.

41.Cinnamon raisin bread

Makes: 1 ½ loaf
Total prep time: 50 minutes

Ingredients:
- 1 cup Water
- 2 tablespoons
- Margarine
- 3 cups Flour
- 3 tablespoons Sugar
- 1 ½ teaspoons Salt
- 1 teaspoon Cinnamon
- 2 ½ teaspoons Yeast
- ¾ cup Raisins

Directions:
- Add all the ingredients in order given except the raisins.
- Add raisins in on the "add in" beep.
- Bake on "sweet bread" setting.

42. White bread

Makes: 12
Total prep time: 47 minutes

Ingredients:

- 1 cup Warm water
- 2 tablespoons White sugar
- 1 (1/4 ounce) package bread machine yeast (2-1/4 Teaspoons)
- 2 tablespoons Melted butter
- 2 tablespoons Oil (can use 4 tablespoons of oil or melted Butter)
- 3 cups White bread flour
- 1 teaspoon Salt

Directions:

- Place the water into the bread pan.
- Sprinkle the sugar then the yeast over the water; allow the yeast to foam for 10 minutes.
- Add in the melted butter, oil, flour and salt.
- Select the basic or white bread setting and press start.

43.Awesome crusty bread

Makes: 1 ½ loaf
Total prep time: 50 minutes

Ingredients:
- 1 cup Warm water
- 1 Package active dry yeast
- 2 tablespoons Shortening
- 2 tablespoons Sugar
- 1 teaspoon Salt
- 2 ½ cups Flour

Directions:
- Place ingredients in bread machine in the order according to the manufacturer's directions.
- Use the regular bread cycle.

44.Best low carb Bread

Makes: 1 loaf
Total prep time: 50 minutes

Ingredients:

- ½ cup Water
- 1 Egg
- 1 tablespoon Butter or margarine
- 2 tablespoons Splenda sugar substitute
- ⅓ cup Ground flax seeds
- ¼ cup Soy flour
- ¾ cup Vital wheat gluten flour
- 1 teaspoon Dried yeast

Directions:

- Using a 1 pound capacity bread machine, combine ingredients according to order given in bread machine manual.
- Select 'light' browning setting.
- Don't remove bread until it is cooled.
- Cut into slices, and store, covered, in the refrigerator.

45. Hot dog buns

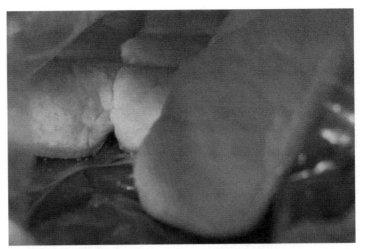

Makes: 12 buns
Total prep time: 50 minutes

Ingredients:

- 1 cup Water
- 1 Egg
- 2 cups All-purpose flour
- 1 cup Whole wheat flour
- ¾ teaspoon Salt
- ¼ cup shortening
- ¼ cup Sugar
- 3 teaspoons Yeast
- 1 tablespoon Vital wheat gluten (optional)

Directions:

- Place all ingredients in bread pan, select dough setting, and press start. (vital wheat
- Gluten is optional but the bread will rise higher with it.).
- When dough has raised enough, the machine will beep.
- Remove bread pan, and turn out dough onto a floured countertop.
- Gently roll and shape the dough into a 12-inch rope.
- With a sharp knife, divide dough into 8 pieces for hamburger buns or 12 pieces for hot dog buns.
- Grease a baking sheet. Roll pieces of dough into balls and flatten for hamburger buns
- Or shape into 6-inch rolls for hot dog buns. Place on prepared baking sheet.
- Cover and let rise in warm oven 10 to 15 minutes until almost doubled.
- Preheat oven to 400°f bake 10 to 12 minutes until golden brown (be careful mine
- Cook pretty fast). Remove from oven and cool on racks.
- When ready to use, split buns horizontally.
- These will keep in plastic bag in the freezer for 3 to 4 weeks.

46.Parmesan bread

Makes: 2 loaves
Total prep time: 50 minutes

Ingredients:

- 1 ½ cups Water (or more, as needed)
- 4 cups Flour
- ¼ cup Parmesan cheese
- 1 ½ teaspoons Salt
- 1 teaspoon pizza seasoning
- 1 teaspoon Garlic powder
- 2 ½ teaspoons Yeast

Directions:

- Add ingredients in order suggested by manufacturer.
- Mine is water first, then flour, then seasonings and cheese, lastly yeast.
- Run on basic or delay cycle.

47. Oat-honey bread

Makes: 1 loaf
Total prep time: 50 minutes

Ingredients:
- 1 cup Water
- ¼ cup Honey
- 2 tablespoons Vegetable oil or 2 tablespoons canola oil
- 3 cups White bread flour
- ½ cup Oatmeal, uncooked
- 1 teaspoon Salt
- 2 teaspoons Active dry yeast

Directions:
- Combine ingredients in bread maker per the manufacturer's instructions.
- Enjoy

***Note: cook time is for the basic/white cycle (medium crust; 1½ lb loaf)

48.Hawaiian bread

Makes: 1
Total prep time:1 hour

Ingredients:

- 3⁄4 cup Pineapple juice
- 1 Egg
- 2 tablespoons Vegetable oil
- 2 1⁄2 tablespoons Honey
- 3⁄4 teaspoon Salt
- 3 cups Bread flour
- 2 tablespoons Dry milk
- 2 teaspoons Fast rising yeast or quick-rising Yeast

Directions:

- Place ingredients in bread machine container in order directed by manufacturer.
- Cycle: white, sweet, no timer.
- Setting: light.

49.Crusty rolls

Makes: 12 rolls
Total prep time: 50 minutes

Ingredients:

- 1 ¼ cups
- Warm water
- 1 Egg white
- 1 tablespoon Vegetable oil
- 1 tablespoon Sugar
- 1 ½ teaspoons Salt
- 3 -3 ¼ cups Bread flour
- 2 teaspoons quick-rising yeast

Directions:

- Place ingredients in bread machine pan as suggested by manufacturer.
- Choose dough cycle and start machine.
- Upon completion of the dough cycle, remove dough.
- Form rolls, place on a greased baking sheet.
- Cover with a towel and let rise in a warm, draft-free location for 30 to 40 minutes.
- Bake in a preheated 400 degree oven for 12-15 minutes.

50. Garlic cheese rolls

Makes: 24 rolls
Total prep time: 2 hours

Ingredients:

- 1 cup Water
- 3 cups Bread flour
- 1 ½ teaspoons Salt
- 1 ½ tablespoons Butter
- 3 tablespoons Sugar
- 2 tablespoons Nonfat dry milk powder
- 2 teaspoons Yeast
- ¼ cup Butter, melted
- 1 Garlic clove, crushed
- 2 tablespoons Parmesan cheese, more, if needed

Directions:

- Place first 7 ingredients in bread pan and select dough cycle.
- When cycle is finished, turn dough onto a floured countertop or cutting board (use Flour sparingly).
- Gently roll and stretch dough into a 24 inch rope.
- Grease two 8 inch pie pans or one 13x9 pan.
- With a sharp knife, divide dough into 24 pieces.
- Shape into balls; place into prepared pans.
- In small bowl, combine butter and garlic; pour over rolls.
- Sprinkle with parmesan cheese.
- Cover and let rise for 30-45 minutes until doubled.
- Bake at 375° for 10-15 minutes until golden brown.
- Remove from oven, cut apart, and serve warm.

51. Super Sweet bread

Makes: 1
Total prep time: 1 hours 30 minutes

Ingredients:
- 3⁄4 cup Water
- 1⁄3 cup Milk
- 3 tablespoons Melted butter
- 3 tablespoons Molasses
- 2 tablespoons Sugar
- 1 teaspoon Salt
- 1 3⁄4 cups Whole wheat flour
- 2 cups Bread flour
- 2 1⁄4 teaspoons quick-rising Yeast

Directions:
- Add ingredients to bread machine pan in order suggested by manufacturer.
- Use light setting and no timer.

52.Cream cheese bread

Makes: 1 loaf
Total prep time: 1 hour

Ingredients:

- ½ cup Water
- ½ cup Cream cheese, softened
- 2 tablespoons Melted butter
- 1 Beaten egg
- 4 tablespoons Sugar
- 1 teaspoon Salt
- 3 cups Bread flour
- 1 ½ teaspoons Active dry yeast

Directions:

- Place the ingredients in the pan in the order as suggested by your bread machine
- Manufacturer.
- Process on dough cycle.
- Remove from machine, form into a loaf and place in greased 9x5 loaf pan.
- Cover and let rise until doubled.
- Bake in a 350° oven for approximately 35 minutes.

53. Cheddar bread

Makes: 1 loaf
Total prep time: 3 hours 15 minutes

Ingredients:

- 1 Package yeast
- 3 cups Bread flour
- ¼ cup Nonfat dry milk powder
- 1 tablespoon Soft butter
- 1 teaspoon Salt
- 2 tablespoons Sugar
- 1 ¼ cups Water
- 1 ½ cups Grated sharp cheddar cheese (at room
- Temperature)
- ⅓ cup Parmesan cheese
- 1 teaspoon Coarse black pepper

Directions:

- Place ingredients in the machine according to your specific instructions.
- Put the liquid into the machine first, then the remaining inure dents.
- This makes 1loaf at white bread setting.

54.Calzone

Makes:6
Total prep time: 1 hours 45 minutes

Ingredients:

- 1 ¼ cups Water
- ½ teaspoon Oregano
- ½ teaspoon Basil
- ½ teaspoon Garlic powder
- 3 cups Bread flour
- 1 teaspoon Powdered milk
- 1 ½ tablespoons white sugar
- 2 teaspoons active dry yeast
- ¾ cup pizza sauce
- 4 ounces pepperoni, chopped
- 1 ¼ cups shredded mozzarella cheese
- 2 tablespoons butter, melted

Directions:

- Place all dough ingredients In the pan of the bread machine in the order by the manufacturer suggestion.
- Select dough cycle.
- After cycle ends, roll out dough on a lightly floured surface, forming a 16 x 10 Inch rectangle.
- Transfer to a lightly greased cookie sheet.
- In a small bowl, combine chopped pepperoni and mozzarella(chopped).
- Spoon pizza sauce, sausage, and Cheese filling in a stripe down the center of dough lengthwise.
- Make diagonal cuts 1 1/2 inches separated down each side, cutting within a 1/2 inch of the Filling.
- Brush top with melted butter.
- You can fold over the sides without cutting the strips .it will taste just as good, but not look as nice.
- Be sure to seal the edges well with water.
- Bake at 350 degrees until ready.

55.Black forest bread

Makes: 1 loaf
Total prep time: 2 hours 15 minutes

Ingredients:

- 1 1/8 cups Warm water
- 1/3 cup Molasses
- 1 1/2 tablespoons Canola oil
- 1 1/2 cups Bread flour
- 1 cup Rye flour
- 1 cup Whole wheat flour
- 1 1/2 teaspoons Salt
- 3 tablespoons Cocoa powder
- 1 1/2 tablespoons Caraway seeds
- 2 teaspoons Active dry yeast

Directions:

- Place all ingredients into your bread maker according to manufacture.
- Select type to a light crust.
- Press start.
- Remembering to check while starting to knead.
- If mixture is too dry add tablespoon warm water at a time.
- If mixture is too wet add flour again a little at a time.
- Mixture should go into a ball form, and just soft and slightly sticky to the finger touch. This goes for all types of breads when kneading.

56.Brioche

Makes: 7
Total prep time: 1 hours 30 minutes

Ingredients:

- 1 3/4 teaspoons Active dry yeast
- 1 3/4 cups Bread flour
- 2 tablespoons Bread flour
- 3 tablespoons Sugar
- 3/4 teaspoon Salt
- 2 Whole eggs
- 1 Egg yolk
- 1/4 cup Water
- 2 tablespoons Water
- 8 tablespoons Unsalted butter

Directions:

- Add all ingredients except the butter to your bread machine in the order suggested by Manufacturer and process on the basic bread cycle.
- Cut the butter into tablespoon size pieces.
- About 10 minutes before the end of your first kneading cycle, begin adding the butter, 1 tablespoon each minute.
- Do not rush it.
- Let the machine continue its process.
- After bread is baked and at the end of the entire cycle, let the brioche cool in the Opened machine about 20 minutes.
- This will keep the sides firm while the center stays moist.

57. Tomato basil bread

Makes: 1 loaf
Total prep time: 2 hours 15 minutes

Ingredients:

- 1 (1/4 ounce) package active dry yeast
- ¾ cup Warm water
- ¼ cup Fresh basil, minced (substitute with 2 Tablespoons dried)
- ¼ cup Parmesan cheese, grated
- 3 tablespoons Tomato paste
- 1 tablespoon Sugar
- 1 tablespoon Olive oil
- 1 teaspoon Salt
- ⅛-¼ teaspoon Crushed red pepper flakes
- 2 ½-2 ¾ cups Bread flour

Directions:

- In a large mixing bowl, dissolve yeast in water. Stir in all other ingredients to form stiff dough.
- Place in a greased bowl, turning once to grease top. Cover and let rise in a warm place until doubled, about 1 hour.
- Shape to form a round loaf.
- Place on a greased baking sheet then cover and let rise until doubled.
- cut the shape "x" in top of loaf.
- Bake at 375° until golden brown.
- Remove from pan to cool.

58. Garlic bread

Makes: 1 loaf
Total prep time: 2 hours

Ingredients:

- 1 cup Warm water
- 1 tablespoon Butter
- 1 tablespoon Powdered milk
- 1 tablespoon White sugar
- 1 ½ teaspoons Salt
- 1 ½ tablespoons Dried parsley
- 3 teaspoons Minced garlic or 2 teaspoons garlic powder
- 3 cups Bread flour
- 2 teaspoons Active dry yeast

Directions:

- Place ingredients in the pan of the bread machine in the order recommended by the manufacturer.
- Select basic bread cycle; press start.

59.Caramelized bread

Makes: 2 loaves
Total prep time: 3 hours 15 minutes

Ingredients:

- 1 tablespoon Butter
- 2 Medium onions, sliced
- 1 ¼ cups Water
- 1 tablespoon Olive oil
- 4 cups Bread flour
- 2 tablespoons Sugar
- 1 teaspoon Salt
- 2 teaspoons active Dry yeast

Directions:

- Melt butter in skillet over medium-low heat. Cook onions in butter 10 to 15 minutes, stirring occasionally, until onions are brown and caramelized. Do not hurry the process. Remove from heat.
- Place all remaining ingredients in bread machine pan in the order recommended by the manufacturer.
- Set to basic cycle with medium or light crust.
- Add onions at beep signal or 5 to 10 minute before end of kneading cycle.
- Alternatively, use dough cycle.
- Remove dough at end of cycle, shape as desired, place on cornmeal-sprinkled baking sheet and let rise. Bake for app. 30 to 40 minutes in a 400 deg. Oven.
- Exact time depends on shape.

***Generally substitute one cup of whole wheat or rye flour for one cup of the Bread flour. Rye is particularly excellent.

60.Cheesy Jalapeno bread

Makes: 1 loaf
Total prep time: 1 hours 15 minutes

Ingredients:
- ½ cup Sour cream
- ⅛ cup Water
- 1 Egg
- 2 cups All-purpose flour
- 1 teaspoon Salt
- 1 ½ tablespoons Sugar
- ¼ teaspoon Baking soda
- ¾ cup Grated sharp cheddar cheese
- 2 tablespoons Seeded and chopped fresh jalapeno peppers (about 3 peppers)
- 1 ½ teaspoons Active dry yeast, for all bread machines

Directions:
- Place all ingredients in bread pan in order according to your bread machine.
- Select light crust setting and press start.
- After the baking cycle is over, remove bread from pan,
- Cool on a rack before slicing.

ABOUT THE AUTHOR

JOANNA COOPER is a leading dietitian, as well as face yoga master, who devoting her life to discover the easiest ways to stay young and beautiful, which means having a good body shape, being healthy and proactive. While living in the United States with her husband Joanna likes to experiment and try new things. After finding out the effectiveness of different diets, she wants to share the knowledge with others and show that keeping healthy lifestyle can be both easy and delicious at the same time. Throughout the whole life, she tested various diets, from undemanding to very strict ones. In fact, as stated by her, the most important thing is to have recipes you can rely on, in such case the word "diet" loses its frightening meaning. Joanna wants people to stop being afraid of trying new things and experimenting with different diets while searching for the most suitable one. That is why she started putting best recipes on the paper, so later everyone who willing to have a collection of the most delicious and already tested recipes could easily find them in one book.

CONCLUSION

Thank you for purchasing this book! I hope this book was able to teach you how to make the best homemade loaves with your bread machine. There are plenty of bread recipes to choose from depending on your taste and the occasion. You might feel a little daunted at first, especially if you have never baked bread in your life, but with a bread machine, there is little to worry about. From a novice, you'll soon be making and baking your own specialty bread in no time.

Happy Baking!